Shadows of Existence

An Anthology of Poetry

Jekwu Ozoemene

iUniverse, Inc.
New York   Bloomington

iUniverse books may be ordered through booksellers or by contacting:

iUniverse
1663 Liberty Drive
Bloomington, IN 47403
www.iuniverse.com
1-800-Authors (1-800-288-4677)

*Because of the dynamic nature of the Internet, any Web addresses or links
contained in this book may have changed since publication and may no longer be
valid. The views expressed in this work are solely those of the author and do not
necessarily reflect the views of the publisher, and the publisher hereby disclaims
any responsibility for them.*

ISBN: 978-1-4401-6119-3 (pbk)
ISBN: 978-1-4401-6116-2 (cloth)
ISBN: 978-1-4401-6118-6 (ebook)

Library of Congress Control Number: 200993406 9

Printed in the United States of America

iUniverse rev. date:08/13/2009

Contents

Foreword

Shadows of Existence started off as a collection of the first few recorded faltering literary strums of my mind activated by Professor Karen King-Aribisala's reading of D. H. Lawrence's "Snake" in her Practical Criticism class of 1993 at the Department of English, University of Lagos, Nigeria.

That reading turned out to be the "open sesame" to a vast region of fecund literary thoughts and dreamscapes and also initiated me to the art of poetic language, its sounds, rhythm, and metre, and the kaleidoscopic world of metaphors.

What you are about to read are some of the floundering thoughts of a boy-man, a step ahead of the age of majority (tottering on the brink of adulthood), and that of the man, grappling with the frustrations and depressions of the adult world, in a grim battle with the strange vagaries and vicissitudes of life and seeking answers to the numerous questions they pose.

Jekwu Ozoemene

Port Harcourt, Nigeria

June 2009

Shadows of Existence

If we do not swiftly set forth at dawn
Dusk is but a nanosecond away
A brief flicker on the skin of time
Concentric ripples racing to distant bays

If we dare tarry to set forth at dawn
We will laze away the thief-of-time
A marathon transformed to a tragic dash
As your day is done and your dirge is sung

"A community leader" obsequious voices intone
Of an innocuous tiny hamlet in the heart of Edo?*
For others, the funeral parlour tidbits scream
A leader! A global citizen! He lived a dream!

We truly must set forth at dawn
To make the best of the dregs of our days
Emerge from our current shadows of norm
And banish the lingering nightmares of our today

We should cast aside our fears
And take life by storm, the bull by the horn
Let's get them to sing this sweet dirge when we are done
He lived! Oh yeah, he sure set forth at dawn!

For me, I will live my true dreams
For dusk beckons
And make the best of this fading light
So that men will say, "He lived life; he surely did live right!"

2008

*Edo   is the dominant tribe in Edo State of Nigeria.

For We Will Live

We will not walk slowly into the dark!
For the night rules only for those who will not fight
We will not lose this fight with night!
For with our bare hands we shall uproot the fright
We will not tolerate prejudice
But will bear and share the pain
We all stand firm against stigma
For in discrimination there is no gain
We will shine forth the light
And fully stretch forth our arms
To welcome our kin

We will live
Together
In brotherhood
In love
HIV not to put asunder
We will not discriminate
For fear of one another
As the more we stigmatize
The weaker our resistance

We hold in our collective hands
The one shot that will win this war
The real vaccine

This day we all decree
That we will live
Together
We will love!
One another
This ... this will be the new creed
By which we will live

2008

My Hourglass

My hourglass trickled away
The sands of time hummed a tune of wasted years
The sands ran out slowly
Until tiny granules of yesteryears
Became sand dunes of sadness
Ugly dust heaps of pain

My patience exhausted
My endurance stretched to the nth
Yet my sandglass trickled on and on
Ever so slowly, ever so slowly

I could have picked up this thief-of-time
My beautiful road-weary sandglass
And cast it far away
Deep into the turbulent ocean currents
To drift listlessly wherever the ocean goes

But supposing
Supposing the ocean harbours more sadness
More pain
More uncertainty and no gain

I think I will rather wait
And reap whatever my hourglass brings
No matter how late

2008

Pyrrhic War

You have tested my armour
Best-of-class sturdy steel
Impenetrable
And has been so from the crack of dawn

You have seen my steel
Icy cold molten fire
Curvy scimitar of gold and sapphire
Carving/slicing through the front lines

I have been slashed
By steel meant for others
Whizzing past my soldier's ears
Deflected by my erstwhile general's fright
To lodge in my reliable Velcro vest
And even that, when his flip-flops
Tested my loyalty ... primed my fears

You sent me up mountains
Down ravines
Always in the heat of battle
Always in the thick of the fray

Soldiers, soldiers everywhere
Fallen by the wayside ... defecting
Standing shoulder to shoulder
Heaving as one body, heaving and pushing

Then ... "Attack! Attack!" was the battle cry
"Ahu! Ahu!" the rugged soldiers would reply

I still relish the trenches, you know
Those little adrenaline pumping slivers of memory
The pungent sting of cordite
The putrid stench of gangrene
Strongly sweet pong of sweaty men
Whine of bullets ...

Then I soaked it up you know
Fear ... the pressure ...
The heat, especially the heat

These are memories I cherish
A life I used to love
Lived to live
But long to loathe

Now I am weary
Very weary
From fighting your fights
Battling your fears

Now I'm tired
A battle-weary Pyrrhic general
Shell-shocked and punch-drunk
An artefact
A curio war relic
Reminder of wars won and lost
Of souls dining in Valhalla

Now I am finished
Ready to be shipped home to an ever-waiting wife

2008

Reflections

Ignited
By the warmth of my sheets
Aglow with the heat of your visit

Memories
Of you rekindled
Like the eternally glowing embers of the stars themselves

Your touch
That incessant teasing caress of a playful butterfly
Sending tremors of sensation to remote digits of my being

Your kiss
That overflowing cup of sweetness
Emanating from a pair of luscious lips
Ever smiling, ever loving

Could it be
That you were here in flesh and blood
As I roll over, immersed in your innocent eyes
Wrap my arms around the thought of you
And waltz with you into the night

2008

Death

When death is a woman
She comes
A surreptitious bride
At clandestine hours
Shy
Of bright lights, noise, and applause
Nibbling slowly at your soul
Taking her time to pick
The unlucky groom of her choice
Begging, teasing, and caressing
Cajoling, smiling, insinuating
Gently sucking life
Into the vortex of her tranquil embrace

But when death is a man
With cymbals and brass drums
Alone or in clusters
In bedrooms or boardrooms
He strides in like a tempest
Smashing, destroying, capsizing
Threatening, swamping, abducting
Stalking death after death
Capturing lives after lives

1996

Lost in Translation (Diaspora)

For those that cannot eat
The palm kernels we crack
Nor chew it with the same vigour
That our forefathers did
For those that cannot sieve through
The residue of our regurgitated pap
Sweet pap the stomach throws up intermittently
And those in the know sweep up swiftly

For those incapable of garnishing their speech
With that age-old palm oil
Or of coating their palate with that time-tested honey
For those that wait in vain under the friendly Udala* tree
In a futile attempt to garner its fruits
Spoils meant for "sons of the soil"

Is it not for them the Ekwe* beats?
And the town crier shrieks himself hoarse
Nor for them the homebound egrets cry
And the cattle moo a sombre remorse
Not for them the yam seedling sprouts its shoots
And roast corn's aroma wafts through the homes of all

Nor for them the Agaba* bares its ferocious teeth
In a macabre dance in the village lawn
Is it not for them the early cock crows
Awakening every home with its shrill bugle?
Nor for them the village belles swing their hips
As they rush through the day's chores

Why not take a trip home
To drink from the stream's sweet fullness
And dance in the therapeutic rainfall?
A trip home
To listen to the rhythm of the blacksmith's forge
And gyrate to the tune the flutist's calls
A special trip home
To thread along those moonlit paths again
And reminisce on loves that surely there began

1997

*Udala   A very sweet, pearlike African fruit.

*Ekwe   A wooden gong known to be used by traditional Igbo
            town criers, which also serves as a musical instrument.

*Agaba   A ferocious masquerade of the Igbos of eastern Nigeria.

As the Walls Come Crumbling Down

The sound of the tiny raindrops fall
Pity-Pata! Pity-Pata! A dirge of wasted matter
Washing away a decade-long mascara
Tracing rivulets of grime on your corrugated "shit"

Rejuvenated by the strength of desire/this ambition
Brushing aside your carefully woven cotton candy
Stolen steel visor that tunnels to your labyrinth
A kaleidoscope of now jaundiced dreams

How deep the rabbit hole goes
Smack into a palace of perfumed putrescence
A dungeon crawling with fellow journeymen
Pockmarked field, cataract-disoriented sight
Each dreamer's vision more blurred than the last

Freeeee! Now I can see
Further than you ever wanted me to see
Deep into the crevice of your wart-lined arse
Away from the odoriferous fumes of your royal fart

No Hero here, no Prophet, no Prince
A conjurer maybe, a wayfarer, a go-for-glory King

Free at last as the wall comes crumbling down
Dust yet to settle, grit in my teeth, yet free
Horizon blurred, a jungle, a jumble of what can be
But the truth is this field is mine
A minefield, yes, but still my field
No Heroes here, no Prophets, just me and my dreams

2009

Totem Poles and the Fraud of Patriarchy

For centuries you have been fooled, wool pulled over your eyes
Covering your ears, down to your modern-day designer shoes
Propelled by orchestrated culture, folklores, and beliefs
Designed to batter your self-esteem, glue them to the soles of your feet

An elaborate myth that has made it difficult for Men
To admit to any lack of skill or knowledge of the art of sex
So Man, as innately selfish as only man can be
Turned nature's dual carriageway/carnal pleasure to a one-way street
Pleasure for Man but for woman a passive retreat
Backed by socio-religious and cultural decrees

That the fraud has survived this long to say the least
(That sex is Man's preserve, Man's right, but a woman's disease)
Is ridiculous, a subject for legends, folklores, and comic relief
He proclaimed that your sexuality is the death of chastity
(So off with your Totem Pole, the centre of craving, they decreed)

Alas you have once again been sold down the river
By a Man incapable of articulating emotional desires
(Aside from the belief that he harbours a raging bull in his pants
Of which all women will pine or faint at its sight)
Trust me, he knows your Totem Pole stands solitary guard
Perched, not inside, but on the lintel of your tavern's arch
And that to achieve relief the Pole, most times, should be worshiped
In consonance with the oftentimes savage in and out thrusting
If you disagree, then Man should practise what he preaches
And amputate his glans (not the foreskin that is useless)

And you Mothers, why arrange to have your daughters amputated?
To think this safeguards your children from society's disdain?
Ordained by a patriarchal community that has since upheld
That man-child can roam and romp the streets at will
(While pre-marital chastity for woman is a rule)

We know that on this, death bell's knell tolls from the body count
Of women dead at parturition and from infections' hands
Yet they play on the fact that Mothers will rather die
Than subject their daughters to society's hue and cry
So off to the butcher's slab they are forced to go
To be initiated into this bloody, needless, and unhealthy code

While Man ensconces himself in an irrational fear
Women routinely endure the invasive male gyno's grope
(He will rather die of prostrate affliction than have a rectal probe)
How Man is Man with a dysfunctional strobe?

At this point I must alight from a bus not truly mine
As the wheel should be manned by sisters, mothers, daughters, and wives
Now the torch is lit, your final female suffrage battle in your hands
Yours to end, yours to stamp out when you desire
This fraud is Man made so that Man can stand at will
Let the Rosa Parks sit so that this curse will forever remain still

2009

Learned Helplessness

My loving husband hovers around the blood-speckled gurney
As I lie, humbled
Spluttering behind splintered Prada sunglasses
Yet he still hovers
Concern tracing the delta of crow's-feet dancing around his flickering eyes
Doctors, Nurses, charmed by his worry, his physique
His tears flow freely, salty pinpricks of deceit
Sliding down his cheeks, glistening on my wedding band
Tiny tear freckles on his bare feet, blood on his manicured hand
His clipped British accent, staccatos, fluid responses to their demands
Beautiful Nurses sway, kowtowing to his spoken and silent commands

As this surreal scene unfolds, I retreat within myself
A soul, stripped of self-esteem, verbally raped and haemorrhaging red
Hyperventilating, me needs to get a grip on me
Where am I? Alive or lying with the dead
Take stock as I try to plan my next move in my head

I drift into flickers of darkness, a cinematographic vortex of memories
The blue-black eye and ruptured eardrum
Bloodied nose and cigarette burns
Cracked jawbone and hairline fractures
Eyes wide shut

Cracked skull and whiplashed torso
Hair pulled out, follicles bleeding
Bandaged elbow wrapped in a napkin
Eyes wide shut

"Is anyone home?" My soul cries out
I shudder, shiver, suddenly cold, all alone
Drift deeper, tumbling, cartwheeling into the warm murky gloom
I have done whatever he proposes, I whisper to no one

But he reverts with beatings, slaps, kicks, and more blows
At first, I thought this love, punishment for my transgressions
Now it's obvious he will have beaten me regardless of my professions
(The first beating harbinger of torrents of successors)

As I struggle back into a reluctant hazy consciousness
He is there smiling, holding my hands, lovingly whispering my name
Then I gurgle, I hear him shout, "Doctor! I need a Doctor here!"
I smile back, head spinning, and sink back to the warm murky depth

In our patriarchal society, across social class, religion, or colour
Traditional belief holds that husbands own their wives (lock, stock, and barrel)
And those women should conform to an ideal of self-denial
Battered, butchered, raped, they cannot petition

Subjected to any excruciating stimulus, they can't escape
They become submissive and reluctantly accept their fate
The earlier this stimulus is received and accepted
The longer it will take to overcome self-deprecation

I once heard that Man's first written societal laws
Proclaimed a sentence for women who verbally abused their lords
Their names to be "engraved on brick," a thick slab of stone
To be used to dash out their teeth, cleaved from cheek to bone
And since this 2,500 BC declaration
Wife-beating has been accepted by various races and nations
From Ancient Greece to the conquering Romans
Jews, Christians, Muslims, and Pagans
Even the much-celebrated French king Napoleon
Decreed that women be treated as "life-long irresponsible minors"
19th century British law states unequivocally
That a husband has "power and dominion over his wife"
And can beat her with a stick "no thicker than his thumb"

I resurface gasping, struggling through a mountain of pain
As tears cloud my eyes, my head throbbing, life fading away
The Doctor arrives and pries open my eyes
His flashing penlight tenterhooks searing my aching cornea
In desperation I summon the last strength from the pits of my stomach
Clutch his collar, and whisper hoarsely in a racketing gargle
"My loving husband, standing by your side, did this to me
It may be too late for me, but you may just save another victim"

2009

This Distressed Heart

The anguish of this distressed heart
Is a burning conflagration
A raging tempest
An obstinate whirlpool of pain

The anguish of this distressed heart
Flows ... a river of red molten lava
That haunts and hoots
Like the owls nocturnal call

This heart, this recipient of untrammelled pain
Has to go on and on
Beating its incessant tattoo
From day to day
From dusk to dawn
To the encampment of willing ears
Tales of glory
Within its sturdy heart
Tales drab and gory
Willing pain behind a veil of deceit
And entwining woe in a yarn of glory

This heart
This heart writhing in agony
Does it have to go on and on
Like an itinerant griot?
Or should it
Should it seek to rest its drumsticks
Seek to cease the pain?
The unacoustic strumming

Or better still,
Should it
Pull down the walls
And let the populace hear the bloodcurdling tales of years gone by?
Will this relieve it of its anguish
This nerve-racking pain?

1995

Death in God's Name

What will you do
If faith marches on your estate?
Your home "spoils"
Gift of an alien God
What casts the die that spawns your birth?
Your birth? Your death?
Or the erratic life-race of an ebullient sperm
So what?
You are born of a faith
Luck, quirk of fate, providence, or lineage?

Yet in God's name, centuries of blood has been shed
Nine primitive Christian Crusades
Tens of modern Muslim Jihads
"God wills it," they scream!
"Death to the infidels," they cry!
Guiles, orchestrated guiles
Spun to kill in God's name

Blood, tons of blood
Spilled and splashed on this historic soil
Jerusalem the crown jewel, a ding-dong prize
Crusaders, Saracens, Jews
All spitting the same semantic vile
Cleverly twisted age-old Abrahamic mazes

I will not tread this course
(for meandering are the paths they preach)
I refuse to dredge the long-dragged dregs of our bestial society
For I know
Deep down in my soul I know
That all vituperations, all guiles
Point to one immutable end of the cosmos
A primary point
Long tainted by racial difference
Cratered boils of different temperaments
And soured rancid broths of hate

Our Church, Our Mosque, Our Synagogue
Our Jerusalem!
The point has been abandoned, long forgotten
Little wonder you fight
Over the right to the elusive mythical light

2008

We Are Man

I will not proselytize for I'm not a preacher
Neither is this filthy fishing for I'm no man's whore
But I'll speak of the life I've lived
Of the life I love, even though I may someday be proved wrong

For we cannot but speak the things which we have seen and heard
For we cannot but wring out the truth
In the midst of myths and legends
We will intricately unravel the bits of our history
Excruciatingly interwoven between bones and echoes of the dead

Please! This arrogance called Man is one
Just one out of Earth's more than one million species
His sole distinction
An uncanny ability to control and thrive
Rivalled by an indefatigable desire and ability to destroy

Our galaxy is one, just one solar system
In over 250,000 uncharted sister galaxies
Our Sun is one, just one
In the Milky Way's glittering galaxy of over a hundred billion suns
In which our Earth is a four-billion-year-old infant
And on which 4,000 years ago
You, Man, espoused your Abrahamic faith and beliefs

So, my dear, now we have the facts in black and white
Let's not argue who is wrong or right
Do you believe yourself wise enough
To call the shots on matters you know not much?

What do you know of nature's conundrum Dark Energy?
Or Dark Matter, the even more befuddling sister mystery?
Ever heard of the "Red Tide Phenomenon"?
Nature's vehicle for truncating the arrogant dominator's tenor
Your socio-religious postulations I'm wont to believe
Just Mass Mentalism to secure the frightening World you see
You are as much in the dark as the very next guy
As the more you learn, the more answers our world desires

So repeat after me, my dear Mr. Man:
We are not and have never been the Universe's anointed
For there have been many who have lived and died before us
We are Man
Earth's dominant specie of the time
A miniscule portion of this unknown dot in the night sky
We are Man
Notoriously known to have made wrong calls in the past
Ask Columbus, ask Galileo
They almost paid the price
We are just what we are, Man
Don't be scared

2009

Dandy-Pastor (Have You Been to Church Lately?)

Have you been to church lately?
For our Dandy-Pastor's nuptial vows
As expected, he cherry-picked from the good Lord's vineyard
Who, but the dashing, urbane, sexy, and witty
Not for him, Mgbeke* or Ugly Betty!

Have you been to our airports lately?
Dandy-Pastor acquires a chariot of fire
(Not for the Lord's chosen a vehicle for hire)
To whisk him in a whirlwind up to heaven
Thirty-three thousand feet above mere mortal's level
(Thirty-three million dollars worth of pleasure and opulence)
No-skin-pain, our rich God's work is worth such indulgence

Dandy-Pastor, whose chariot is this, I'll like to know
Speak out now or we'll rant, smite the waters, fast from now till
tomorrow
Others will whisper, "Who made him King?" behind their sleeves
But that will achieve or end nothing I believe
A tenth of our earnings feed his lifestyle
That's why the sin-chariots will fly daily across the night sky
Probably ferrying the lovely Bathsheba
While poor Uriah bleeds to death on the frontlines

Whose glamorous garment is this anyway?
The same garment that healed by touch, for free, no pay?
Or could the cost of his exquisite English Tom Ford
The broad-shouldered couture of his German Hugo Boss
Hand-tailored garments of French Yves St. Laurent
Provide Medicare to thousands of his pitiable flock?

Christ! Whose mercantile church is this anyway?
All yee vassals to swashbuckling buccaneers
Is this the Lord's vineyard that we were all promised
Or the Tithe Collector's awe-inspiring fiefdom?

So I ask again
Have you paid your tithe lately?
For Dandy-Pastor's chariot needs more fire
Mummy's wardrobe a new attire
And the Good Lord's vineyard
Leeched, withering away, left to die

2009

*Mgbeke   A traditional Igbo name for the female gender. Used colloquially to represent a local, ugly female.

Eyes & Fingers

Eyes that can see what others cannot write
Stare boldly where others dare not peep
Fingers that will write what others dare not see
Fiery cold lines that linger when others are long dead

Fingers and eyes to transcribe my thoughts
Into monuments of time and a heart
As hard as steel to stand the heat or chill

1997

Golgotha's Laughter

Patriotism we thought we heard
Greed they sought to shield
"Crucify him!" they screamed as one
A Caesar he has become
For who crowned him King unto us
A pretender he is to our trust

Some sought a head on a platter
While some Golgotha's laughter
But all seemed to concur to the fact
That the pretender's seat was bound to crash
To dethrone the King they sought as one
So Barnabas rose to the clarion call

The King he crested Golgotha's height
As his eerie cold laughter rent the cold night
He glanced at his guards with a wry smile and shrugged
As the centurions fought to wrench his hot spot
A dice they choose to pick his fate
His garments they rent through rabid fisticuffs and hate

Barnabas they knew so they shoved him aside
To choose a new pretender who will fight for the dice
"Crucify him!" they screamed
As they cast lots and fought
For Caesar it was who crowned Barnabas at night
Again, his eerie cold laughter was heard through the night

As they scrambled and fought for the loot they siphoned
A thunderbolt struck and dispersed them for home
For the old men of yore had foretold this grave date
That even if a Caesar dies, another will rise from his grave

1993

Hell's Gates

Darkness steals away the day
As the guests retreat in a flurries' haste
But we are bound to our perilous post
As the winds march past at a furious pace

I long to lie and hug my cot
And watch the angry raindrops duel the wind
As they meander through Sango's* bolts of light

To think that Heaven's gates are just ajar
And the sky erupts its bowels in scalding rain
What if Hell's gates are flung open?
Blood and brimstone will surely flow

Let the rainmakers be prevailed upon
To keep Hell's gates firmly locked for all

1993

*Sango   Also known as Shango or Xango in Latin America, Sango
             is the Yoruba (western Nigeria) god of thunder and
             lightning.

Saprophyte—The Almajiri's* Cry

When push comes to shove
We get mowed
For you
Insured by your air-conditioned fortress
Never espy the gory battlefields

When shove comes to heave
We get slain
For justice is your design
Loopholed to justify your whims and desires

When "Jaw-Jaw" erupts into "War-War"
Foreign havens await your siblings
And for us
Death's bell's knell taunt our offspring

Yet we fight
Long-drawn battles with hunger and starvation
We fight
Our life's blood oozing to Hell's damnation
On we fight
With Hell's gates flung open
You—the demon
We—the damned

Our lost souls mournfully hum that hunger is our anger
So on we fight
Your pieces of silver lubricants to our lubricating gastric juices
On we fight
Till our hunger fed anger doused
Then we rest
For now

2008

*Almajiri   Child and teenage beggars, usually found in the major
cities of northern Nigeria.

Facebook Valkyrie

Facebook Valkyrie
Guardian of cyber Valhalla
Whose enclave have you infiltrated?
Who have you maimed?

On the face of your book
(this lovely book of your face)
New preys lurk in your crosshair
Married, marinated ... lonely
Mostly lonely
All tomorrow's victims of your lure

Facebook Valkyrie
Odin's stalker of the lonely nights
You should know that I have fought many battles
Won many wars
On land, sea, of the heart and in the spirit

For me
A Valkyrie will be but a minor skirmish
A trivial adventure to wet my battle-axe
Catch me if you can

2008

Amidst the Wheat Stalks

Your cicatrised chest taunts you
A mockery of the folly you commit
Blade-lacerated features
A reminder of your beliefs
The ash impregnated pap
Sits, an unholy burden, brewing in your insides
And your fingernails
Still smart from your last unholy manicure

The cock crows
An invective at your injustice to their kind
Lizards, bats, dread your approaching footfalls
Afraid of your lurking shadow
Your rivulets of amulets
Beat an ominous tattoo
Heralding your malfeasant approach
And on your being
A pervading ambiance of evil
Fouling the earth's airspace

Why mock the pew by your weekly visitations?
Why ridicule the Book with your papal recitations?
What right have you to claim this faith
(To challenge my lack of faith)?
By day a saint, at night a demon
Venomous weed growing freely amidst the wheat stalks

1996

Another Challenge

Shoulders heavy, mind desiccated
Only my resolve propels me
The thought of failure blows a fanfare in my eardrums
Edging me on
Till exhausted
I arrive at the spring
And what a spring
Banked by beautiful flora and peopled by bubbling crystals
All full of life

Deep droughts I drink
With the fecund moisture flowing down my face
Over my chest and seeping as far down as my weary soles
Finally
Homebound I stride, saturated
With the sun's furnace bathing my brow
Awaiting
Yet another challenge

1997

Tall Gorgeous Ebony

Velvet black ebony dermis
Proportionate tall serene lady
Arouse my thoughts of your sensuous being
Anytime I look at thee

2008

Night Bus

Winging through the rough gullet of the night
Ferried by spirituals, choruses of hope and prayers
Driven by a common factor
Fear!
Of the dark, cold night
Fear, of the luxurious metal contraption
Fear, of our myriad of fears
Fear, gut-wrenching fear

Yet we all sit
Some praying, some singing
Some sleeping, others silent
All willing the road's appetite
It's hideous "Machine Cutter"
To ignore us, to bypass us
For its teeth are sharp at night we all seem to think
Especially at night

Night bus, do you know
If we'll live to see the sunrise over our heads?
If I'll ever hear the rhythm of the blacksmiths forge again?
If we'll see tomorrow?
If tomorrow will ever come?

But the night bus hurtles on
Its only answer an ominous whistling fart
The journey is long it seems to say
The night is very long

1996

Songs of Success

Broken pieces of cowry
Scattered on my dreams
Jagged slivers of silver
Shattered my beliefs

Whatever turn I took
The same talons flailed me ceaselessly
With whatever step I made
This same adversary, this same horror
Taunts me incessantly

In my slumber
Shrieks of "pieces of eight"
Haunt me till date

Yet I still envisage
The year of the full cowry
I anticipate
A money monsoon
I dream of dreams to kill this corpse
Of nightmares where the corpse gets to walk
Dreams and dreams that satiate my resolve

So we will tread the pathways
That several have trudged before
We will scale the mountains
Trim those talons
And make them mere playthings
Soft paws of velvet

Then
Only then will we sleep
With songs of success swelling our hearts

1997

The Road To Tinkom-Tinkom*

Remember ...
The old psychedelic path to Tinkom-Tinkom
Poppy fields of orchestrated madness
Ecstatic route to a pulsating paradise
Songs of silver ringing in our ears

Well, all that is history now ...
For I stand on the track to Tinkom-Tinkom
Buffeted by the North-American-Trade-Wind
Hurling shards of a juggernaut

On both sides ...
Abacus ringing, knuckles cracking
Cymbals clashing, markets crashing
Decimated pieces of "Pieces of Eight"

We stumble ...
Through a maze of toxic molten lava
Amidst the dead and dying
Journeymen to ... lifeless senseless ruins ...
Ruins, as far as the eye can see ...
Ruins

In search of a detour to Tinkom-Tinkom?
A loose thread
That unravels Midas' wonders

So off we go again
Finders' keepers!
Wading through chasms of chaos
Senseless toxic sub-prime assets
In search of a path ... the new detour
Another race to Tincom-Tincom ...

2008

* Tinkom-Tinkom   Tinkom-Tinkom, or Itom Kom, is the mythical
                         land that appears in various Igbo folklores.
                         Legend has it that it lies somewhere between
                         the land of the living and that of the dead.

Your Yellow Brick Road

What drives your dreams today?
Is it the illusionary tinkling of silver
Or the cold steel glitter of gold?

What drives your dreams today?
Is it the dreams that you dreamt about yesterday
Or the nightmares smothering you today?

Whatever propels your dreams
Each man to man his cyclone
Tenaciously ride its fury

To lead him gently
Onto the Yellow Brick Road
His very own Emerald City

Or he can leave the rudder unchecked
Blindly steering through the unfriendly seas
Back to the great grey Kansas prairie

2008

Morning after the Wedding

Mama said I must get married now
That there is a groom for every girl
Now lying on this wedding bed
Beside this puny creature and his balding head
With the early morning sun rays, the guests long gone
(A-Listers, Pantheon of local belles)
Left with a room filled with useless gifts
Cheap blenders/throw pillows/all epitome of thrift

Bills! Bills! Bills! and more bills
A million naira, a wedding reception hall full of glitz
Spent, wasted, gone, a sunken cost!
Our coffers empty, our pockets lined with dust

Now the singing and dancing is long done
The in-laws and out-laws have since be gone
Our coffers dry, our lawn full of trash
All I am left with is this emptiness of a man

Mama said I must get married now
That there is a bride for every man
"Maybe you are not looking hard enough," Aunty Tarry said
"You must be haunted by an ancestral spirit, a husband from the dead"

"When will you marry?" my mama said
"Tuesday or Wednesday, or when I'm dead?"
A complex maze of Brownian human hormones
Impinging on a thousand years of societal notions

Mama said I must get married now
That my mates are long past their childbearing prime
For her counsel I have this being that I now call my own?
And what in hell did I see in him at all?
("You are getting old!" my mama shrieked.)
That is why, I guess
I have ended up in this mess
(But how come those outside are dying to get in
To be trapped in steel bars, society's psyche?)

Mama said I must get married now
That my mates are long past their childbearing prime
But his touch is clammy, the feel of dead fish
So sex, romance is clearly not my wish
This marriage is a prison and off to jail I go
So a strong front, fabricated lies to keep my woe my own

"How did I manage to get here?" I ask
Lying by this snoring snorting man
Will he pummel me every day?
Or will he cheat on me and still make me pay?
Will I cheat on him in this new life of deceit?
What does my darling Mama say to this?
(You will grow to love him, she pleads
You can change and mould him, Aunty Tarry cedes)

Should I get myself a toy-boy for my needs?
Or a prosthetic man tool, a vibrating drill
For the real marriage begins the morning after the wedding
After the guests are long gone and the bank account is in red
Help! For I truly cannot stand this man by my side
Now, what will my all-knowing Mama say to that?

2009

That Ancient Rhythm

The wind blows across the horizon of my mind
As I play back my astral cassette
Carefully savouring the blissful moments we spent in each other's arms
I remember your smile
That ancient treasure
Which veils the secrets of your tender years
As you slowly shed that synthetic veneer
Created to satisfy the morals of the pious
They billowed around your feet like waves washing around a yacht at sea
Your skin ...
Slippery to my touch
As flesh met flesh and lips met lips
And at the thought of your lips
My soul awakens
And lo! You are before me
Lips to lips
Hips to hips
As we swing away to the rhythm
That ancient rhythm

1993

Our Desires

Where do I start my search in this maze of light?
Where do I rest my oars to my heart's delight?
When and where will our souls snuggle close and waltz in unison
To cupid's sweet melodies and our hearts' sweet throbbing?

Only where you want it to be
Only when your heart says it should be
At the point when your eyelids dim with love and desire
Your twin-lakes ablaze with light, with my fire
Only then will I snuggle close
Only then will my fingers transverse along these shores of delight
Only then can we ignore life's declivities and acclivities
And sleep
Cocooned in our desires

1997

Pilferntrophist

Irritatingly fat rotund creatures
Strolling-rolling in complacency
Oblivious of the hostile glances
Irked by the sweating faces

Burrowed furrowed creased brows
Puckered squirming uneasy bows
Men await Midas' gift of grace
To ease life's turbulent tumultuous race

Bulbous rich putrescent "mine"
Spewing wealth and life's decline
Sherwood Forest from ages recesses
Reincarnates in their jolly faces

Mouths agape, we sit and await our cake
Banked and baked in this modern rape
Awaiting the surely descending manna
From the Tuareg to the peasant farmer

What right have they to dictate the pace
And delve out ours through their erring grace?
Those clapping hands and shrieking calls
Sure signs of their impending falls

1994

Mona Lisa/Cloning You

I've tried to capture your beauty
To grace the sands of time
I've struggled to ensnare your ambiance
Decipher your science
To benefit generations yet to come

All I want is for their malleable nascent minds
To nourish on your uniqueness
To inhale the fire that courses through your unique design

But I've failed
Just like several before me
For only his fearful hand and eye
Can frame these immortal symmetries
Only his fire, only his forge
Can recreate this wonderful creation

1996

A Tuneless Rhythm

How does one dream for a nation
That was built without a vision
When insomnia squats
A deadly sentry at his bedpost

How does one claim patriotism
When jingoism has become an aberration
And egocentrism the password of the nation

Why should one die for a country
When death is a resident citizen
Convalescing on streets stalked by pestilence and annihilators?

Soothe a weary people
(Console a bereaved nation)
When its founding fathers chastised it with whips
And the present gatekeepers with scorpions?

From whence will the messiah come
When blood brothers are killing blood brothers
And mothers vilifying their daughters?

How does one weep for a people
Whose tear glands have been ripped out
And hearts replaced with a block of stone-cold steel
Whose sweat glands have been cauterised
And bodies corrupted on its unholy brew
Whose oil glands have been desiccated
And mind and skin saturated with fear?

But we will still cry for our visionless state
(A stateless vision)
We'll ever remain patriotic to the crimes and labours of our heroes past
We'll march on and on to the tuneless rhythm of our leaders' band
Till we drop off one by one or the leaders realise the time's demands

1994

Cura-Cao

Tender sprout of Eden
Still alien to the age-old feeling
Of nubile tarts and prurient hags
Now regretting their bidding

Enticed by the rhythm
At fifteen you were rearing
(A lamb on a tether)
To have your field's play

Morality discarded with frivolity
Materialism in an intercourse with eternity
Innocence seceding from virginity
The dictates of a new day

Pomposity veiled complacently
Your anatomy a field amenity
Accumulating talent in your waist
Your God's gift debased

Intimacies accelerate your nemesis
At par with the wild's carnivores
To be consumed like a carnivore
Is your life debt to pay

1993

Here Comes the Pain

If your scion have lived through interesting times
Ravaged by the travails of boisterous storms
If your radicles have encountered radical tempests
Marooned ashore barbaric shores

If you have lived through your children's wailings
As frenzied gastric juices
Gnaw away at the empty stomach walls
Assailing the bowels with a thousand afflictions

As evil and sinister temptations
Claw frantically at a paranoid mind
Transmogrifying friends into fiends
Monsters into masters

A time when excogitations desiccate a fertile mind
Masticating it into autonomous boluses of putrid paranoia
When the body becomes an "ATM" of survival
An ugly license to lucre licentiousness

When the most intrepid of men
Shrivels like a salted earthworm
Shrank by rigor mortis and a raging sun

Then
Only the early memories will soothe the beleaguered soul
Cleanse the putrefied spirit
When the pain comes (as here comes the pain!)
Only the good sweet memories will serve
As the Anodyne of present pain

1995

Weather Report—Apocalypse

Minor showers on Earth?

Not at all
Hoofbeats of an impending storm
Galloping chargers of a looming doom
Apocalypse ...
Death ... Pale as ever ... Apocalypse

Sunny in Hades today?

You wish ...
Only White ... majestic White
Of the bow and arrowless quiver
Crowned king of war and famine
Cantering, drumbeats of a conqueror
Death, starving death ...

So it could rain in Hell tomorrow?

Thunderous downpour of hunger and starvation
Red ... swirling, long swathes of violence
Famine, mass starvation, and death

We will FRY on earth today!
For death, the Black rider rides!!
Fuel, food, and financial crisis
(Not forgetting fertilizer, food of the soil)
Desiccating our homestead ...
Decimating our land ...
"Run, Forrest, Run!"

2008

Of Homes & Hearts

From two hearts devoid of love
A poisoned home devoid of warmth
From this warmth-less heath
A robbed generation
Plundered of the essence of life
Built on hate and hurt
Bound by fragile trust and broken hearts
Resting on a foundation of pulsating lies
A fragile bedrock of pain

But why?
Why should a home be devoid of warmth?
Why should two hearts be devoid of love?
Why should a tender generation
Be mortgaged by deceit?

Why should these young hearts
Grow on sour milk and stale broth
On rancid rancour and rabid conflict
On progressive hate and conflicting lies?

Even after the storm
The scars of yesteryears
Live within the earth
Pulsating
Waiting to erupt

1995

Adam & Eve (Woman Talk, Man Talk) I

Those empty boasts of theirs are vain
Inducing sleep like pouring rain
So quick to prove their budding wealth
Peddling lies (possibly disease) that could ruin your health
It's ridiculous, and I really wonder why
These little boys will elevate themselves so high
We double in laughter at those funny thoughts
Of the lengths these boy-men will go to court

Will Adam never learn his lesson?
Ever eager to taste Eve's apple of Eden

Adam & Eve (Man Talk, Woman Talk) II

They dine with us and play the fool
And pretend that they are pretty cool
The more thought I give it, the more I wonder
Why this façade should turn us on
For those things they say to cause us hurt
Are actually meant to make us court

Should God review the case of man
And society permits an Eve stalking Adam
The yoke will ease and we'll step aside
And watch the game from another side
Will Eve play the game our way
Or rewrite the lines to make us pay?

1993

Rendezvous

From afar I spy her approach
Bathed in the mellow-warm glow of the amber candlelight
Like a small mellifluous yacht she rides the waves
Regally, as she sails to my small alcoves height

I rise and hug my queen's sweet warmth
As we sit as one and I hold her tight
Oblivious to the wine and "à la carte"
We drink our lips and warm our hearts

As one we float away like swans
So white, so pure our love thus soars
Across the seas and back to shore
We traverse the world and relish our tour

I pinch myself to rest assure
That mine is real and not a hoax
But she is right in front of me
As serene and lovely as only she can be

1995

Sermon from the Rock

Mace, crown, sceptre, throne
Onus of the people's hope
To love and mind
To house the guide
Through conflict and confusion's drone

Men will seek to crest your height
Via polling booth or martial might
When cocooned with the people's rights
They man your crest to crown their fight

Teacher, farmer, soldier, spy
Uneasy is he who holds you tight

1997

Africa Is Not a Country, Lagos Is My Song

My hotel choice was strategic
Conveniently close to my getaway umbilical cord
The ant-colony bustling Heathrow Terminal 5
A brisk short walk to the domicile of my prey
An urban-jungle shopping arcade
Boisterous by day, eerily quiet and lonely at night

A brief glance at my timepiece
Tick-tocking regally towards the appointed time
And then, on the stroke of the hour
The building's sphincter splits open its seams
Spewing forth a motley spray of gaily dressed credit-crunched teens
Adults and more teens in jeans
An overflowing concrete jungle, medley of tribes, colours, no greens
Immigrants, global citizens hurrying to catch a bite
Before the conveyor belts start the roll into the long night

My earlier text message crisp as the hotel's linen bedsheet
"Will wait for you by noon, nice bar at the end of the street"
A brisk short walk from my expensive hotel suite
The rendezvous
To meet a neighbour's-cousin's-neighbour's-daughter I'm yet to meet

We must have recognised each other within the same heartbeat
She with her green and white striped apron and coy funny hat
I in my couture fitted shirt and Armani slacks
Beaming an Oscar-winning beam I reserve for this act
I pull her off the street
Into the warm embrace of the dimly lit bar
The eager warmth of her clothed skin searing through the defence of
my sheepskin gloves
Our orders danced off the à la carte like notes off a song
And off pirouetted the protective gloves and wary smiles

A tall glass of lager, an espresso, and two sulking muffins
Then bla! bla! bla! bla! and more bland blabbing
Steady power, decent transport, people's power bla, bla, bla
Teeth clenched, ears plugged, five minutes vocal torture, raving mad
She almost got away with it, until she uttered the sacrilegious words
"So when are you back to Africa?" I hear under the silent roar
Jaws droop, eyes widen, forced jaws shut with a thud
Look of incredulity a dead giveaway, mad, why mad?
"What did you say?" the "ay" in my "say" dragging on and away
"If you meant Nigeria that will be tomorrow not today"
Her response an "Awwwh" followed by a partially suppressed giggle
With a heave of her barely clad chest followed by an almost feline wriggle

It's a continent of 53 countries, I scream in my head
Her response, a tilted Igbo babble I barely heard
Like a confluence of a thousand indigenous African tongues
Spoken from the matrix of humanity, voice of all songs
Africa's womb of which bore the womb that bore her grand mum

Peals of laughter tinkled forth, bobbing the funny hat atop her braids
"Awhright," she sighs and cocks her cute little head
I quickly fumble in my pocket, pulling out a wad of rumpled bills
And mutter, "From your folks, greetings from Nigeria to these barren hills"
I mumble a hasty goodbye and beat a retreat to the cold street
The still full glass of lager a still-silent witness to my exit

Back to Knightsbridge, back to my cozy hotel suite
The Asian doorman bows with a flourish and pulls open the door
"Nice weather today and please mind the wet floor"
"I hope you stay the week for this weather will surely hold"
I wince as my umbilical cord to Lagos shivers in the cold
Bed tonight for me and back to Lagos tomorrow my man
He shrugs as if to say he has tried all that he can
I almost scream, Africa, Lagos Nigeria here I come!
A humongous herd of humanity, a paradise baked in the sun
"Ohhh Lagos Nigeria," I sing like a love song
The doorman's look says, "There goes another mad one"
Nigeria is my country, just thought that you should know
Africa is not a country, but Lagos is my song

2009

To Santa, My Christmas Wish

The Yuletide has sneaked upon us again
And for the children and childlike
Who still believe
Santa's gifts is their bargain

So I wish for something special
A sensuous gift I have longed for
Dreamt of all my life
A simple gift of great complexity

I wish for someone
Pretty, witty, and loving
Who can give as much as I give
And take as much as I take
Someone who knows where I ache
And when I hurt
Who cares and can share
And bear my miseries
Who will partake in my victories
And not flare up at my inconsistencies

For the sake of this
And only this
I become like a child once more
Nose pressed against the frosty windowpane
Praying that Santa's sleigh will bring home
My Little Princess
Home to roost
Home were she truly belongs

1997

The Christmas Tree's Song

It's so lonely out here
With blizzards roaring and storms howling
With the winds rustling my leaves
Raging to strip me bare to my soul
Cold and very lonely it has been for me

The thought of Christmas
Brings warmth and joy
For I will once again be bedecked
In gay colours and frills
And the thrills of a traditionally effervescent Christmas spirit
Keeps me warm
Especially when I envision our future
A house full of love, laughter, and joy

But when this Christmas is over
Will I be dumped
Alongside the firewood
Of yesteryears
Shrivelled and dead?
Or will I live forever
In the heart of the one that matters
The one that I care for?

1997

The Sigh of an Angel

Love's song is like an angel's sigh
An enchanting mellifluous melody
Borne on the wings of a beautiful day
Floating high and low
On a Yuletide's lazy Harmattan breeze
Oftentimes leaving quivering quavers,
Quivers full of nostalgic semi-tones
Of bittersweet afterglows

But then the ballad of true love
Is a serenading promenade of purity
A never-ending salsa of togetherness
A cruise of trust, caring, and sharing

Love for me
Is as sweet and pure as a Christmas carol
Sung from the lips of an angel in full flight
Love for me
Is like the enchanting mellifluous melody
Of the sigh of an angel

1997

The Gift of Christmas

Guided by royal beauty bright
The three Kings of Orient
Traversed the land
Heavily laden with exotic gifts
Searching for the mother lode of gifts
The Christ Child's gift

As Christmas draws near
The theme of love
Christ-like love
Rings in our ears

For those who can love
Who do love
True, snow-white universal and untainted love
This is the time to share that gift
The gift of Christ-like love

1997

My Inspiration

I saw a poem
Meant for the eyes and heart
Of my friend's Queen of Hearts
So I felt I should pen this poem
For the Princess of my heart

What inspired what?
Was it the poem on my friend's queen?
Was it the thought of you which has remained with me
Spreading its warmth
Evenly into my Christmas thoughts

The poem or the thoughts
Whichever prompted which
You remain the inspiration of
The creative aspect of my aspirations

1997

About the Poet

Jekwu Ozoemene currently works as a senior manager with Access Bank Plc in Port Harcourt, Nigeria. He holds a degree in English from the University of Lagos, Nigeria, and a specialist MBA in Finance from the University of Leicester, United Kingdom.

In his spare time, Jekwu teaches Project and Real Estate Finance at the FITC (formerly Financial Institutions Training Centre) in Lagos, serves on the Presidential Implementation Committee on Affordable Housing, and acts as a resource person on Mortgage and Title Insurance to the Federal Ministry of Environment Housing and Urban Development Nigeria.

He has written five stage plays: *Nightmare* (1996), *Hell's Invitation* (1997), *This Time Tomorrow* (1998), *Objections Overruled* (2000), and *We Will Live* (an adaptation of *Hell's Invitation* in 2008). Except for *Objections Overruled*, his other plays have been staged on several occasions in Nigeria, all to critical acclaim, though none has been published yet.

Jekwu lives in Port Harcourt, Nigeria, with his wife, Pat, and two children, Kaycee and Kosi. *Shadows of Existence* is his first collection of poetry.

Notes

Notes

Notes